SCIENCE FACTORY

SHAPES & STRUCTURES

JON RICHARDS

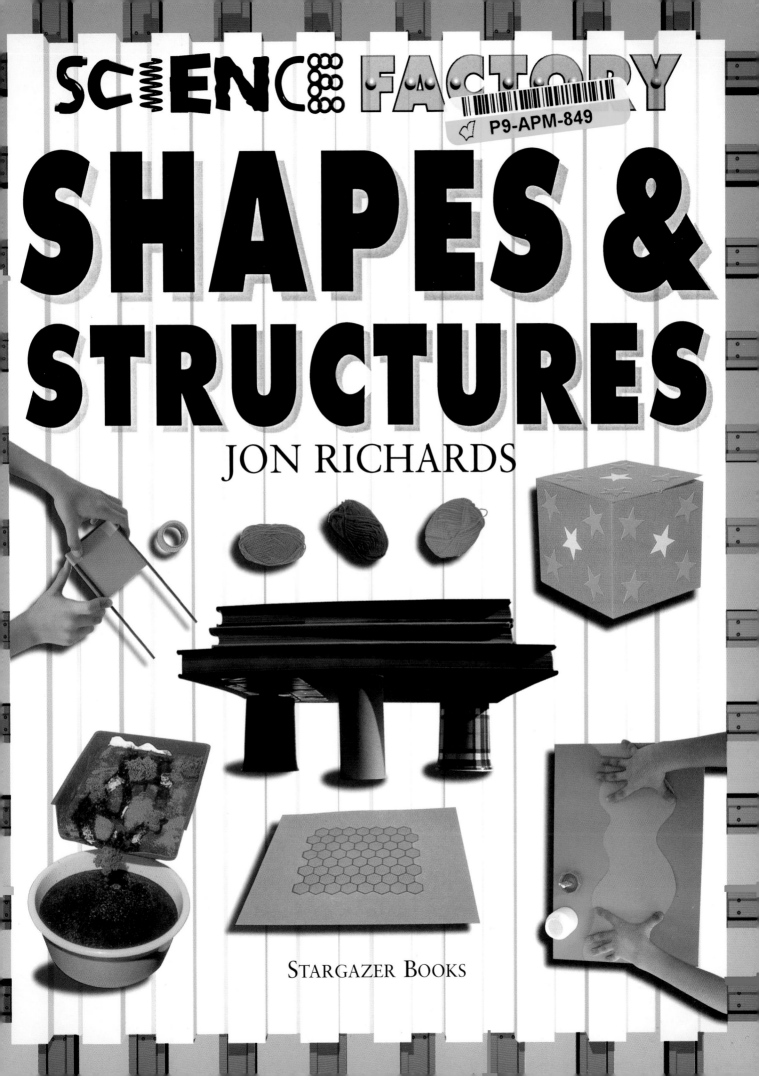

STARGAZER BOOKS

New edition published in 2005

Designed and produced by
Aladdin Books Ltd

First paperback edition published in
the United States
in 2005 by
Stargazer Books
c/o The Creative Company
123 South Broad Street
P.O. Box 227
Mankato, Minnesota 56002

Editor
Kathy Gemmell

Design
David West
Children's Book Design

Designer
Jennifer Skelly

Illustrator
Ian Moores

Printed in U.A.E.

Cataloging-in-Publication data is
available from the Library of
Congress

ISBN 1-932799-69-9

INTRODUCTION

Every object, large or small, has a shape and a structure. Some shapes fit together better than others, and some materials are stronger than others. Read on and discover the properties of different materials. Find out which shapes and which materials are best for building strong structures, such as skyscrapers and bridges.

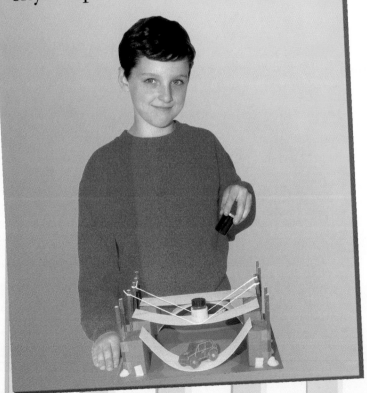

CONTENTS

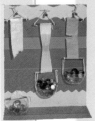

YOUR FACTORY

BEFORE YOU START any of the projects, it is important that you learn a few simple rules about the care of your science factory.

● Always keep your hands and the work surfaces clean. Dirt can damage results and ruin a project.

● Read the instructions carefully before you start each project.

● Make sure you have all the equipment you need for the project (see checklist opposite).

● If you haven't got the right piece of equipment, then improvise. For example, any paper that you can see through will do just as well as tracing paper.

● Don't be afraid to make mistakes. Just start again – patience is very important!

Equipment checklist:
- Large bowl and jug
- Paints and powder paint
- Sand and soil
- Metal and plastic lids
- Wooden disk and wooden blocks
- Modeling clay and model trees
- Toothpicks, saw, and hexagon stencil
- Liquid detergent, bottle cap, wooden spoon
- Paper, colored cardboard, and tissue paper
- Stiff wire, thick wire, weight, plaster of Paris
- Plastic bag, sheet of plastic, plastic tray, and plastic cups
- String, ruler, pens, pencils, coins, and books
- Cardboard boxes, cardboard, and thick cardboard tubes
- Table-tennis ball, empty spray can, and marbles
- Cloth, tracing paper, wooden dowel
- Scissors, tape, and glue
- Colored yarn and pipe cleaners
- Milk, vinegar, and cooking fat
- Saucepan, a sink
- Watch

WARNING:
Some of the projects in this book need the help of an adult. Always ask a grown-up to give you a hand with sharp objects such as scissors.

HANDLING HEAT

WHAT YOU NEED
Toothpicks
Paper
Tape
Colored pencils
Metal lid
Plastic lid
Wooden disk
Cooking fat
Large bowl
Hot water
Watch

IN DECIDING WHICH MATERIALS to use when making something, designers and engineers must decide which materials are best suited to a particular job. For example, it would be no good making a saucepan out of plastic, because it would melt as soon as you put it on the stove. Sometimes they may even need to test various materials to find out which works best for the task. This project lets you test several materials to find out which is the best at conducting heat.

FEEL THE HEAT

1 *Cut out three pieces of paper the same size. Tape each piece of paper to a toothpick to make three flags. Decorate each flag differently using colored pencils.*

KEEPING IT HOT

Collect cups made of different materials, such as metal, plastic, and china. Fill each of these with the same amount of hot water. Leave for several minutes. Then, using a thermometer, find out which cup is best at keeping the water hot.

2 *Cut three lumps of cooking fat that are the same size. Place one lump on each of the metal and plastic lids and the wooden disk. Push a flag into each lump of fat.*

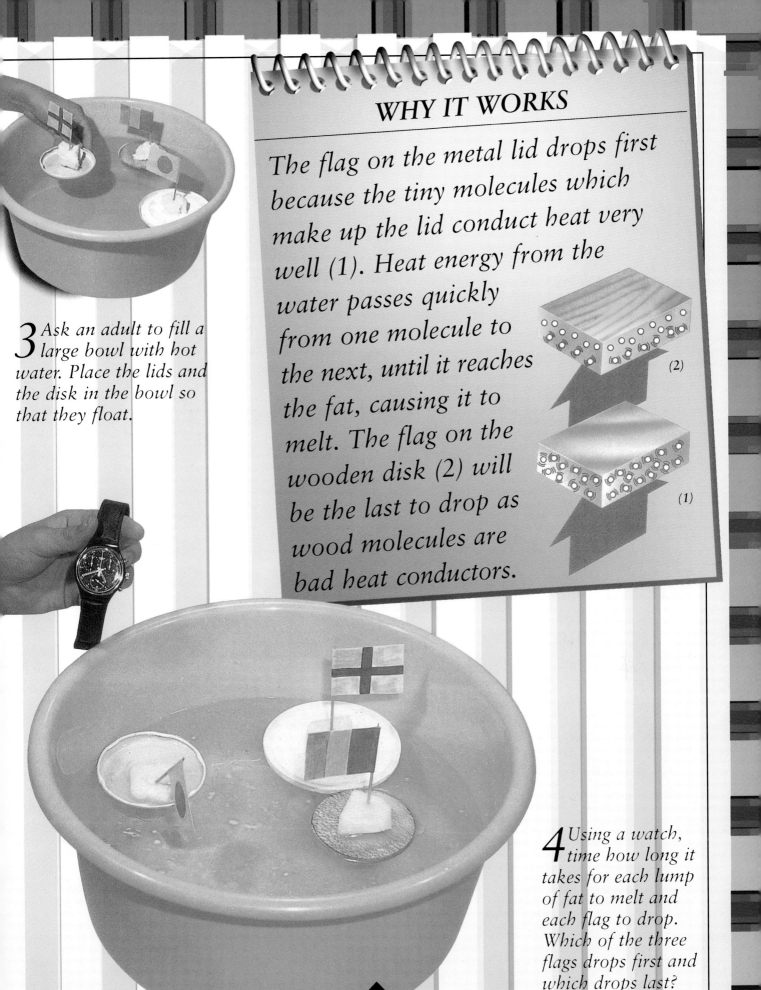

WHY IT WORKS

The flag on the metal lid drops first because the tiny molecules which make up the lid conduct heat very well (1). Heat energy from the water passes quickly from one molecule to the next, until it reaches the fat, causing it to melt. The flag on the wooden disk (2) will be the last to drop as wood molecules are bad heat conductors.

(2)

(1)

3 Ask an adult to fill a large bowl with hot water. Place the lids and the disk in the bowl so that they float.

4 Using a watch, time how long it takes for each lump of fat to melt and each flag to drop. Which of the three flags drops first and which drops last?

TESTING MATERIALS

WHAT YOU NEED
Paper
Tissue paper
Plastic bag
Scissors, Tape
Wooden dowels
Three plastic cups
String
Marbles
Colored cardboard

THE LAST PROJECT SHOWED how to test materials to see which was the best conductor of heat. Another important property of a material is its strength. A material must be strong enough for the job it has to do – one that breaks under the slightest pressure may be dangerous if used for the wrong thing. This project shows how to find which of three materials can carry the heaviest load.

WHY IT WORKS

The plastic bag strip can carry the most weight because the tiny molecules that make up the plastic are held together by very strong bonds. The tissue paper is the weakest strip because it is made up of fibers that are not very densely packed and come apart easily.

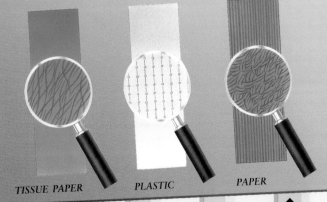

TISSUE PAPER   PLASTIC   PAPER

CARRYING THE LOAD

1 Cut three strips from the paper, the tissue paper, and the plastic bag. Make sure that they are all the same width.

2 Tape one wooden dowel to the top and bottom of each strip.

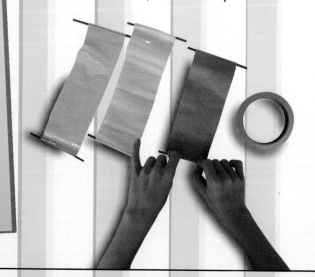

3 Cut some string and tie it in a big loop. Cross the middle of the loop over the bottom of each of the plastic cups and tape it in place, as shown.

4 Loop a cup over one of the dowels on each strip, as shown. Tie another string loop to the dowel at the other end of each strip.

STRIP TESTING

Repeat the test with three strips of different widths of the same plastic. Which carries the most weight?

5 Make a stand from colored cardboard and push three dowels through it, as shown. Hang the strips from the dowels. Add marbles to the cups until the strips break. Which one breaks first?

SPRINGY MATERIALS

WHAT YOU NEED
Stiff wire
Table-tennis ball
Tape
Paper and cloth
Pipe cleaners
Paint
Bottle cap
Cardboard box
Empty spray can
Thick cardboard tube
Scissors

YOU MIGHT HAVE NOTICED that some materials, no matter how much you stretch, crush, bend, or twist them, will always go back to their original shape and size. Sometimes it is important to use flexible materials like this. For example, a plane's wings are designed to bend a little to absorb the force exerted on them by flying. This project lets you have fun with a material's flexibility.

JACK-IN-THE-BOX

1 Make a spring by coiling stiff wire around the empty spray can.

2 Paint a face on the table-tennis ball. Tape a pipe cleaner to the bottom of the ball for your Jack's body. Make a hat from some cloth.

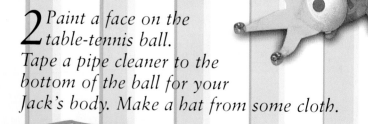

3 Tape the bottom of the pipe cleaner body to a bottle cap. Tightly wind one end of the spring around the bottle cap. Use pipe cleaners to make arms. Make clothes and gloves from cloth.

4 Decorate the cardboard box using the paints.

5 Tape a short piece of the thick cardboard tube to the bottom of the box. Make sure the spring fits snugly inside the tube.

WHY IT WORKS

Most materials have elasticity – they can resume their shape after being squashed. In a spring at rest (1), all the forces acting on it are balanced. Squeezing increases the forces that make the spring want to spring apart (2). Releasing the spring causes it to push apart again.

(1)

(2)

HANGING DOWN

Fix a weight to the end of a ruler. Hang it over the edge of a table. Now move the ruler so it hangs further over the edge. Does it bend more?

6 Put the spring inside the tube, then push the jack down into the box, and close the lid. Open the lid quickly and watch the jack spring up out of the box.

MAKING PLASTICS

WHAT YOU NEED
Milk
Saucepan
Vinegar
Paints
Wooden spoon

THE LAST PROJECT SHOWED you how to make metal wire elastic by coiling it into a spring. But some substances do not return to their original shape when pulled out of it. These are plastic substances. Wet clay is plastic because you can mold it into any shape and it stays that way. This project shows how you can turn everyday ingredients into a plastic material.

PLASTIC POT

Place a plastic yogurt cup in a saucepan. Ask an adult to pour boiling water over it. Watch as it loses its shape.

PLASTIC MILK

1 *Ask an adult to slowly warm some milk in a saucepan.*

2 *Just as the milk is starting to bubble, slowly stir in some vinegar.*

WHY IT WORKS

When the vinegar is added to the milk, it starts a chemical reaction. This causes the tiny molecules that make up the milk to clump together. Instead of being runny and free to move, as they are in the liquid milk, the molecules form one large lump. This lump is your plastic material.

MILK MOLECULES
CLUMP TOGETHER

3 Keep stirring and adding vinegar. Within a few seconds the mixture should turn rubbery.

6 Decorate your plastic with the paints.

4 Once it has turned rubbery, let the mixture cool. Ask an adult to put it in the sink.

5 Ask an adult to put some of the cooled mixture on a plate. Run it under cold water until it is completely cold.

SHAPING MATERIALS

PLASTIC MATERIALS CAN CHANGE SHAPE without returning to their original structure, as you saw when you made a plastic substance in the last project. Plaster of Paris is a substance that can take on the shape of any container or mold it is poured into. It starts as a powderlike substance that can be mixed with water to form a paste. The paste then sets hard. This project shows you how to mold plaster of Paris.

WHAT YOU NEED
Cardboard
Tape
Modeling clay
Liquid detergent
Plaster of Paris
Scissors

MOLDING SHAPES

1 Ask an adult to make a frame out of cardboard. Tape it to another piece of cardboard, as shown. Make a pattern out of modeling clay in the base of your frame.

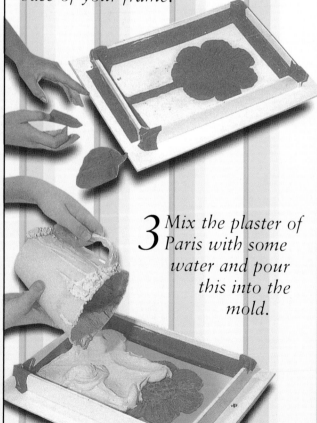

2 Cover the modeling clay shape with liquid detergent. This will stop the plaster of Paris from sticking to the modeling clay.

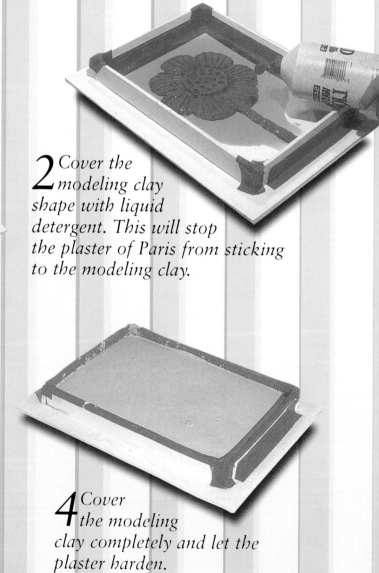

3 Mix the plaster of Paris with some water and pour this into the mold.

4 Cover the modeling clay completely and let the plaster harden.

WHY IT WORKS

When plaster of Paris is mixed with water, it forms a paste that can be poured into a mold. Over time, the water evaporates (goes off into the air as a gas) and the paste hardens to form a brittle substance.

PLASTER OF PARIS

WATER

5 When the plaster is dry, gently remove it from the frame. You will see that the plaster has hardened with the shape of the modeling clay set into it.

PLASTER PICTURES

Use your mold to make shapes from modeling clay. Simply press the clay into the plaster and it will take on the pattern of the mold.

WEAVING MATERIALS

WHAT YOU NEED
Cardboard
Scissors
String
Colored yarn
Wooden dowels

SOME MATERIALS ARE ONLY strong in one direction and so are not good to use in structures by themselves. One way around this weakness is to weave strands of material together. This creates a new structure that has strengths in all directions. Clothing fibers are an example of this. They combine threads to create usable materials. Learn how to weave strands of yarn in this project.

WHY IT WORKS

The strings running up and down your loom are called warp threads. The yarn strands that you weave across the loom are called weft threads. By weaving the threads together, the finished fabric is strong. The closer the weave, the stronger the fabric.

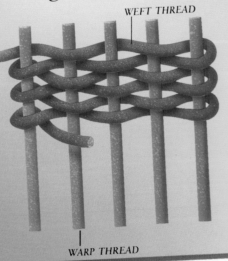

WEFT THREAD

WARP THREAD

SMOOTH FIBERS

Have a look at the ends of different threads of material with a magnifying glass. Compare the sizes of each fiber and see how smooth the ends are.

MAKE A LOOM

1 To make your loom, ask an adult to cut an odd number of notches along the top and bottom of a piece of cardboard.

2 Wind a length of string around each pair of notches and knot each loop at the back of your loom.

3 Weave a strand of yarn in and out of each length of string. Make sure you push each row up into the one above it. To change color, tie your new yarn onto the end of the old strand.

4 When you have finished, knot the last piece of yarn and lift the fabric off your loom. Push two wooden dowels through the top and bottom of your material and hang it up as a decoration.

GETTING STRONGER

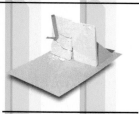

WHAT YOU NEED
Cardboard
Tape
Thick wire
Plaster of Paris
Weight
Scissors
String
Sheet of plastic

SOMETIMES, ONE MATERIAL ON ITS OWN is not suitable for a job, and two or more different materials may need to be combined to create the right material. Fiberglass, for example, contains tiny pieces of glass in a plastic, which makes it both flexible and strong. In this project, see how you can strengthen plaster of Paris by adding another material.

WHY IT WORKS

The block of plaster alone (1) is brittle and will break when a strong force is applied to it. The block that contains the metal wire (2) will last longer because it can bend a little and absorb the knocks it receives.

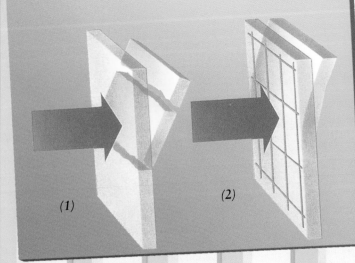

(1)   (2)

REINFORCED PLASTER

1 Use the frame you made and follow the steps on page 14 to make one block of plaster of Paris. (You don't need to make the mold.)

2 When the block is dry, remove it from the frame. You need to make another block the same size, but before you start, lay some pieces of wire into the frame.

CLAY BRICKS

Make bricks out of clay and leave them to harden. Now make more bricks of the same size, but this time mix some straw into the clay. Test them for strength and find out which ones last the longest.

5 *Swing the weight at the blocks of plaster. Make sure that you hit each block at the same spot and that you release the weight from the same distance each time.*

6 *You will find that the block with the metal wire will last a lot longer before it shatters than the block without any wire.*

3 *Lay the wires both across and lengthwise, as shown here. Now make your second block of plaster with the wires embedded in it.*

4 *Ask an adult to cut out cardboard supports and lean the blocks against these on a sheet of plastic, as shown. Tie a weight to a length of string. Tie up the string so that it can swing.*

NATURAL STRUCTURES

WHAT YOU NEED
Plastic tray
Large bowl
Water
Modeling clay
Sand and soil
Green powder paint
Model trees
Saw

SOME OF THE LARGEST and most impressive structures found on this planet are not made by humans at all. Instead, they have been formed naturally by the forces of the wind, sea, rivers, or even the movement of the massive plates of rock that make up the earth's surface. These structures include soaring mountains, enormous canyons, and towering waterfalls. This project shows you how a river can carve shapes and structures into the landscape.

FREEZING WATER

Water changes the shape of the land when it freezes. To see how, fill a plastic bottle with water. Screw the top on tightly. Put it in a sealed plastic bag in the freezer all night. The water expands as it freezes and shatters the plastic bottle.

7 *Slowly pour in water at the back of the tray. Watch it flow down the slope, carving a path into the sand and soil. Make sure you catch the water in a bowl.*

1 Ask an adult to saw off the front of a plastic tray.

2 Put some mounds of modeling clay around the bottom of the tray.

3 Pour the soil over the mounds so that they are covered. Make sure that the soil forms a slope from the back of the tray down to the open front.

4 Cover the soil with a layer of dry sand.

5 Now cover the sand with a layer of green powder paint to give a grass effect.

6 Add some model trees. Make a record of what it looks like by drawing or taking a photograph.

WHY IT WORKS

Water always flows down a slope (1). As it does so, it picks up soil particles and carries them along. The more soil it carries, the more it changes the landscape around it. Some rivers form huge bends called meanders (2). Over time, these bends are worn away, leaving small, crescent-shaped lakes called oxbow lakes (3).

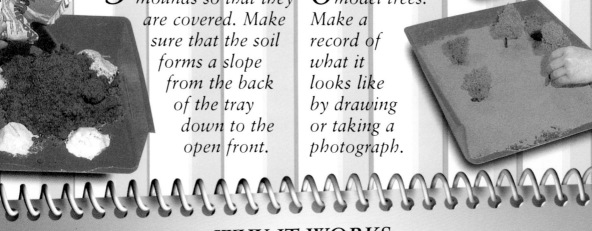

(1) *(2)* *(3)*

21

CHOOSING SHAPES

WHAT YOU NEED
Colored cardboard
Tracing paper
Scissors
Ruler
Pen
Hexagon stencil
Glue

OTHER PROJECTS IN THIS BOOK have shown you how to decide which material is the best for your structure. Another thing that designers and engineers have to decide is the shape of the structure. This project shows how shapes that fit together exactly are good for covering an area or making strong structures.

HEXAGON GAME

1 *Using a stencil, draw and cut out 64 six-sided (hexagon) shapes from two colors of cardboard. Make sure they are all the same size.*

2 *Now stencil onto a piece of cardboard 64 hexagons that tessellate (fit together exactly). Trace the pattern and transfer it onto a sheet of colored cardboard.*

3 *Ask an adult to cut out both patterns and stick them together to make a strong grid. Go over the lines with a pen.*

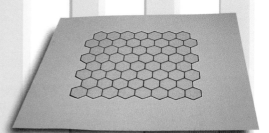

4 *Stick your hexagon grid onto another, larger sheet of cardboard.*

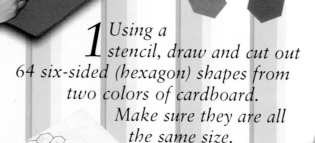

5 *Ask an adult to cut out the shape from cardboard shown here, and fold it to make a small cube. Mark three sides with a 1 and the other three with a 2. This will be your game dice. Ask someone to play the hexagon game with you.*

MAKE A MOSAIC

Use different shapes and colors to make a pattern or picture on some cardboard. This type of picture is called a mosaic.

WHY IT WORKS

Hexagons can cover the board because they tessellate. This means that they fit together exactly without overlapping or leaving gaps. Shapes that tessellate make strong structures. Bees use hexagons to make a honeycomb.

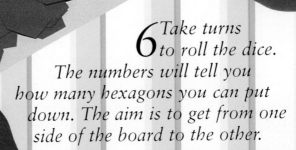

6 Take turns to roll the dice. The numbers will tell you how many hexagons you can put down. The aim is to get from one side of the board to the other.

TESTING SHAPES

WHAT YOU NEED
Two identical cardboard tubes
Coins
Books
Plastic cups

YOU TESTED DIFFERENT TYPES of material for strength on pages 8–9. Strength is also an important factor when deciding if the shape of a structure suits a task. Tessellating shapes are strong and are good for covering an area, as you saw in the last project. This project shows you how some shapes can be strong in one direction but very weak in another.

WHY IT WORKS

The shape of the tube means that it can take a lot of compressional (squeezing) force along its length. However, its sides are weak, and they will collapse when the slightest compressional force is placed on its side.

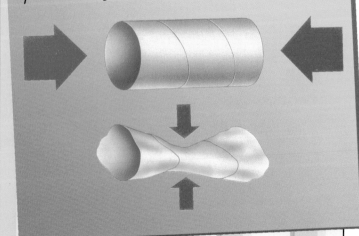

EGG STRENGTH

Repeat the project, but this time use an egg instead of the cardboard tube. You will find that, like the tube, the egg can bear more weight when it is standing upright (you will need some modeling clay to hold it in place) than when it is on its side.

24

TUBE TESTING

1 Place a cardboard tube on its side. Stack coins on either side of the tube, until they are just below the width of the tube itself.

2 Place one of the books on top of the tube. Keep adding books until the tube collapses and the books rest on the stacks of coins.

3 Place the second tube on its end. Put plastic cups that are just smaller than the tube on either side.

4 Again place the books on top of the tube. See how many books have to be added before the tube collapses.

5 This time, you will find that you need more books before the tube collapses.

TALL STRUCTURES

WHEN PUTTING TOGETHER A BUILDING, engineers and designers have to be aware of the stresses and forces that the building might be subjected to over its lifetime. They must then find the best materials and shapes to keep the building upright. This project shows you one solution for coping with the large forces a tall skyscraper has to put up with.

WHAT YOU NEED
Ruler, Pen
Thick cardboard
Colored
cardboard
Scissors
Glue

5.5 inches

3.5 inches

3 inches

1.5 in.

8 inches

3.5 inches

REACH FOR THE SKY

1 *Ask an adult to cut out a number of rectangular shapes from the thick cardboard, using the dimensions shown here. Cut slots in the longest pieces where the dotted lines are.*

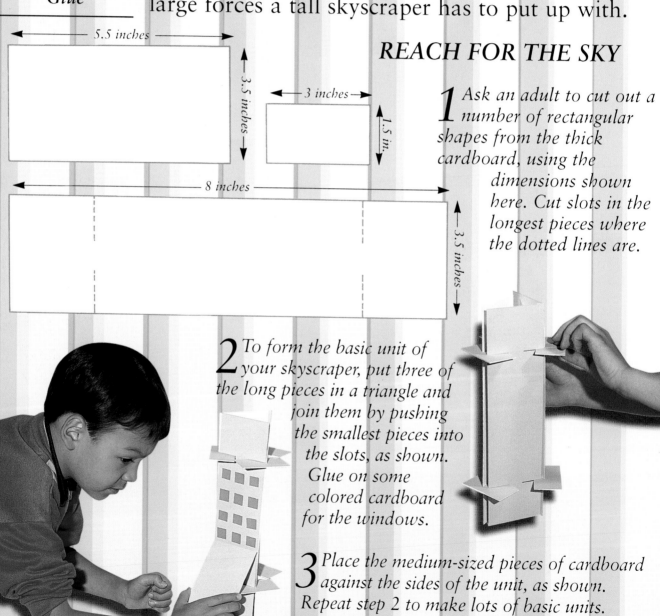

2 *To form the basic unit of your skyscraper, put three of the long pieces in a triangle and join them by pushing the smallest pieces into the slots, as shown. Glue on some colored cardboard for the windows.*

3 *Place the medium-sized pieces of cardboard against the sides of the unit, as shown. Repeat step 2 to make lots of basic units.*

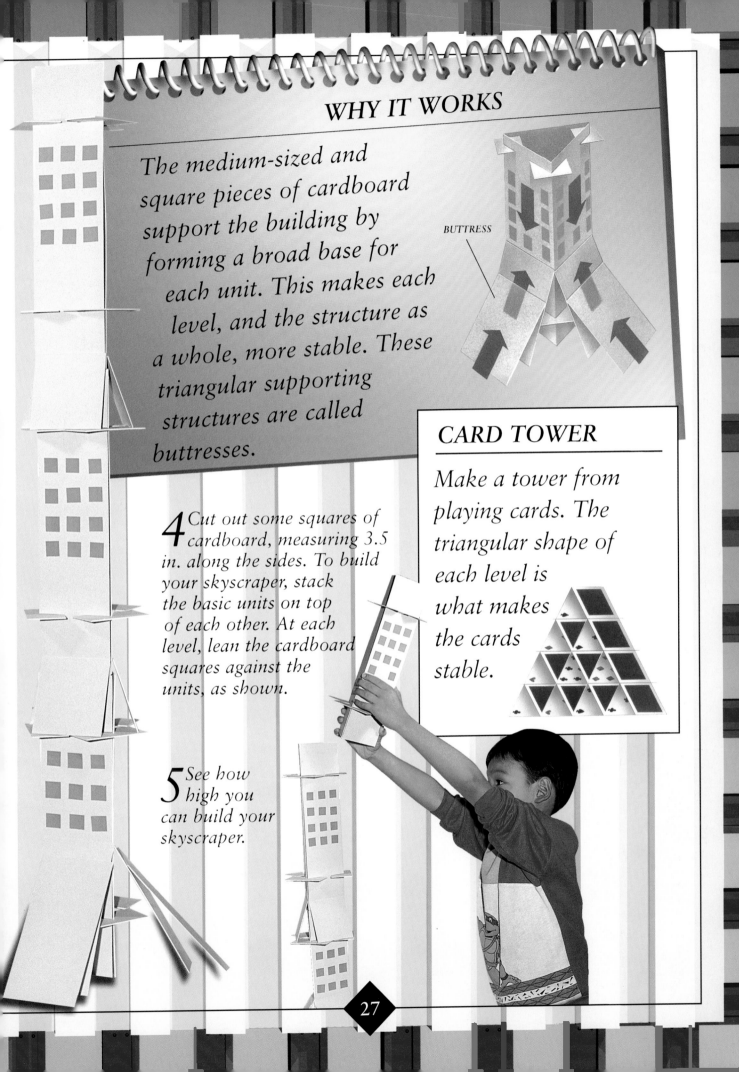

The medium-sized and square pieces of cardboard support the building by forming a broad base for each unit. This makes each level, and the structure as a whole, more stable. These triangular supporting structures are called buttresses.

BUTTRESS

CARD TOWER

Make a tower from playing cards. The triangular shape of each level is what makes the cards stable.

4 Cut out some squares of cardboard, measuring 3.5 in. along the sides. To build your skyscraper, stack the basic units on top of each other. At each level, lean the cardboard squares against the units, as shown.

5 See how high you can build your skyscraper.

27

BUILDING BRIDGES

WHAT YOU NEED
6 Wooden blocks
Pencils
Tape
Cardboard
String, Glue
Colored
cardboard
Modeling clay

THE LAST PROJECT SHOWED you how to build upward. But what happens if you have to build a structure that runs across something? Bridges give designers and engineers different problems. This project shows some of the ways that these problems can be overcome.

BRIDGING THE GAP

1 Tape pencils to two corners of each wooden block, as shown here.

2 Ask an adult to cut out strips of poster board the same width as the wooden blocks. For the first bridge, simply place one strip between two of the blocks.

3 For the second bridge, tie string around two pencils, and tape it to the middle of a cardboard strip, as shown. Then tie it to the pencils on another block.

CANTILEVER BRIDGE

Another bridge structure is the cantilever bridge. Make your own cantilever bridge as shown here and see how much weight it can support.

4 For your third bridge, place another strip of cardboard under the first strip. Glue this to the wooden blocks and your bridge's roadway to form an arch.

WHY IT WORKS

Your first bridge will buckle quickly as it has no supporting structure for the road. The road held by the string, called a suspension bridge, will buckle next. The strongest bridge is the arch bridge. The arch shape is best at spreading any weight on the bridge over its whole length.

5 Make a river landscape with colored cardboard, as shown below. Fix the bridges to the landscape by pressing the pencils into modeling clay. Test the bridges by placing heavier and heavier weights on them. Find out which one can carry the most weight.

FINDING OUT MORE

ARCH This is a natural or artificial structure that crosses an open area in a curve. *Find out how an arch can make a bridge stronger in the project on pages 28–29.*

COMPRESSIONAL FORCE This is a force that squeezes something. *See how you can test different objects against compressional force in the project on pages 24–25.*

ELASTIC When a material is elastic, it is capable of returning to its original shape after it has been squashed or pulled. *You can find out how to make metal wire elastic in the project on pages 10–11.*

PLASTIC A material is plastic if it can be shaped when it is soft and then sets hard into its new shape. *See how to make plastic material on pages 12–13.*

STRONG SILK

Some of the silk that spiders make, which they use to spin their webs, is actually stronger than steel of the same thickness.

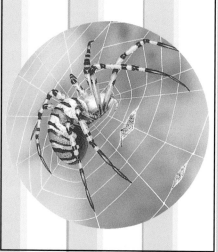

HOT STUFF

The tiles that cover the space shuttle are made from a material that can withstand the high temperatures of reentering the earth's atmosphere.

SKYSCRAPER This is a very tall building usually found in large cities. *Find out one way of keeping very tall buildings such as skyscrapers upright in the project on pages 26–27.*

INSIDE BONES

The bones in your body are not solid. Instead they are full of holes containing bone marrow and blood vessels. This means that they are strong as well as light.

WARP THREADS

These are the threads that run up and down a material as it is being woven. You can learn how to weave your own material on pages 16–17.

SUSPENSION BRIDGE

This uses long cables hung from towers at either end of the bridge to help it take the weight of objects crossing it. *Build your own suspension bridge in the project on pages 28–29.*

TESSELLATE

When shapes tessellate, they cover an area completely without overlapping or leaving any gaps. *Find out on pages 22–23 how you can use tessellating shapes to make a fun game to play.*

WEFT THREADS

These are the threads that run across a material. *See how weaving weft threads through warp threads on a loom can make a material in the project on pages 16–17.*

CONCORDE

The windshield of the Concorde is covered in a very thin sheet of solid gold. This is because gold is very good at protecting the jetliner from the heat that is generated when it flies faster than the speed of sound.

INDEX